Well Red

Liverpool FC in Pictures

Foreword by Tommy Smith
Compiled by Les Rowley

L.F.C.

GRANADA

About The Book

Congratulations. You've just got your hands on *Well Red: Liverpool FC in Pictures*. A unique insight into three decades of the most successful British team ever. Heavy on images and light on words, this book is a tribute to those players who created all the drama on the field and those who caught it through their lenses off it.

Back in the early '70s, the Liverpool team managed by Bill Shankly began an unrivalled campaign of European and domestic dominance. Their rise coincided with growing media interest in football and if anything was written or photographed first, it usually involved Liverpool. This team were the kings of the sport and the club the one that fashioned superstars. Its sense of history is all the more impressive when you consider the club's achievements. One of the things this book salutes is the fact that it took over 42 games, and a few unsung heroes like Ronnie Rosenthal, to win a League title and over a dozen games to win in Europe. Liverpool were much more than a few European matches and Wembley appearances.

With that in mind, the idea behind this book was to have a collection of photographs that sums up the spirit of the team. We have deliberately attempted to stay away from common and much used shots, replacing them instead with rare and previously unpublished pictures that will provoke fond memories for fans, seeing them for the first time. Some are simply quite brilliant and others offer a more subtle suggestion of what went on for all those years on Merseyside. From Bill Shankly consoling the opposition in their own dressing room to Ian Rush celebrating yet another predatory strike on goal. We go to the present crop of stars like Owen and Fowler via the glory days of Souness and Dalglish. Something for everyone.

A book like this has been long overdue and you could say it has been thirty years in the making.

We hope you enjoy it, we certainly did putting it together.

Foreword

When Liverpool Football Club contacted me and asked me to write a foreword for a book they were producing, I asked them what the book was about and they informed me that it was named *Well Red* and it was a pictorial book about Liverpool FC, dating from 1970 to 2000. It didn't take me long to make up my mind and say yes, but I honestly thought that all I would be doing was going through a book that would contain old photographs that had been reproduced over the years in other books, and I would be thanking Liverpool FC plus congratulating the publisher on doing a good job.

Not so. As I read the book I was pleasantly surprised. I can honestly say I had not seen many of the photographs I set my eyes on, before. Memories came flooding back to me of the days when I had the pleasure of wearing the famous red jersey and playing for the team I had supported as a schoolboy. Early in the book there is a photo of Phil Thompson dated 1978, the year I missed the European Cup Final through injury and the year I left the club I had been with for eighteen years. It was a sad time for me, and also for my good friend and team mate Ian Callaghan who had served the club for twenty years. A few pages later I came across the image of Keegan and Bremner being sent off at the Charity Shield game. When was there ever a charitable match involving Liverpool and Leeds? That day they should have called it the 'Uncharitable Shield' – great game, great result.

Next came the memories of the 1971 European Cup and the photograph of Terry Mac's great goal followed by one of Joey Jones, one of the game's greatest characters and one of my best mates (Munchum Joey). What can I say about 1977, it was one of my greatest and happiest memories in my time at Liverpool FC. For the reader, the book contains lots of happy memories of Liverpool FC in the good years – 1970s and 1980s – but unfortunately the football gods have not been very kind to us in the 1990s and the reader must endure some sad memories too.

Having played for the great football people who started the Liverpool FC success story, I would like to add that they and myself wish the present manager Gérard Houllier and Phil Thompson all the luck in the football world in bringing Liverpool FC back to the glory days.

Enjoy the book, enjoy the memories.

Tommy Smith

Spot On

Phil Neal scores the penalty that deflates the whole of the Man City team, including Joe Corrigan.

Riding High

Robbie Fowler makes sure
his goal salute gets seen
from the very back row of
the Kemlyn Road Stand.

Ring...Ring...

'If that's Bryan Robson, tell him
I'll call him back at half-time.'

Fan Power

Fans show their faith in manager Graeme Souness. One month later he was gone.

Sweet FA

Bob Paisley and Chairman John Smith at the FA's HQ in London to defend the club's 'perm' policy. Seriously, they were summoned to explain the actions of Kevin Keegan at the Charity Shield match against Leeds.

Before...

...And After

What a difference
a trophy makes!

They Think It's All Over ...

A defining moment in the club's
history. Who else but the
player–manager grabs the
winner to secure the League
title at Stamford Bridge.

No Pushover

Stan Collymore talks physio Mark
Leather through another exciting
journey up the M6, from his
Midlands home to Merseyside.

Cool Customer

Mark Lawrenson sums up the reception the team received when they ran out at Old Trafford.

previous page:

Table Football

Bob Paisley takes the team through some new variations on the winning theme.

In The Bag

The man signed to replace Ian Rush when he went to Juventus scores the first against Everton at Wembley.

In His Stride

Terry McDermott fires home the first goal
in the European Cup Final against German
side Borussia Mönchengladbach – much
to the joy of the engraver whose job it was
to put the winner's name on the trophy.

Defender Of The Faith

Bruce Grobbelaar weathers a
snow storm against Newcastle.

I Love You Too, Ref

With his boots gathering dust,
Graeme Souness, the manager, has
to let his fingers do the talking.

High Flyers

John Barnes falls head over heels for Arsenal's David O'Leary.

King Of The Road

At a Doncaster petrol station, Kevin Keegan takes a day off from scoring goals to attend the UK auditions for *The Dukes Of Hazard.*

Doh!

Liverpool 0 Blackburn 3.

**Okay Lads,
Here's The Plan**

A final get together to discuss
some match-winning tactics.

In A Rush

Mel Gibson wasn't the only Lethal Weapon. Paul Walsh plays a supporting role as Sergeant Murtaugh.

Berger King

Despite having a bad hair day Patrik Berger and co. had a good day, beating Arsenal 2 – 0.

Standing Room Only

Alan Hansen steps out on to the Anfield turf to receive the League championship trophy in front of a packed house.

Well Worth Watching

No matter where you were, as player or fan, when David Fairclough came on as sub he was one to keep your eye on.

Try These For Size

Bruce Grobbelaar gets spoilt for choice as the boot room sales assistants rush to fit him with a new pair of boots.

Thanks For The Game, Son

As gracious in victory as he was in defeat, Bill Shankly passes on his best in the Bristol Rovers dressing room.

All At Sea

In the bathwater of success, someone up at Liverpool left the tap running!

Liver Birds

Twelve hours slaving under a hot
dryer and a group of female
supporters are ready to follow
the team to another Cup final.

The Real Thing

By moving to Spain, Steve
McManaman has the Bosman
ruling to thank but prays he's
made the right decision. A
Champions' League Cup
Winners medal suggests he has.

A Star Is Born

Goals are his business and
business is looking good.

Tongues Are Wagging

Nice to see Peter Beardsley scoring
off the pitch as well as on it.

In Safe Hands

Ray Clemence clocks on for another 90 minutes between the posts, this time at Elland Road.

Standing Ovation

A reason to celebrate as the team books another FA Cup final place (ominously against Wimbledon).

Tough At The Top

Steve McMahon and
Peter Reid on another
derby collision course.

'What's It Say, Brian?'

'Super Cally scores a
hat-trick QPR atrocious.'

Home Alone

Neil Ruddock, showing the sort of form that packed fans into the Anfield stands.

Walk On The Wild Side

Such was his success nobody
dared question Bill Shankly's
training methods.

Well Red

The attackers' viewpoint.

Fashion Victim

John Barnes, at a 'Save The
Zebra' convention, spots his tailor
in the crowd.

Danger: Low Flying
Silverware

Graeme Souness and Ronnie
Whelan begin their League
championship celebrations
following the game with Spurs.

Walk This Way

This is the traditional time when players walk out at Wembley and look for family and friends in the crowd. All Barry Venison's group seemingly had tickets at the Everton end.

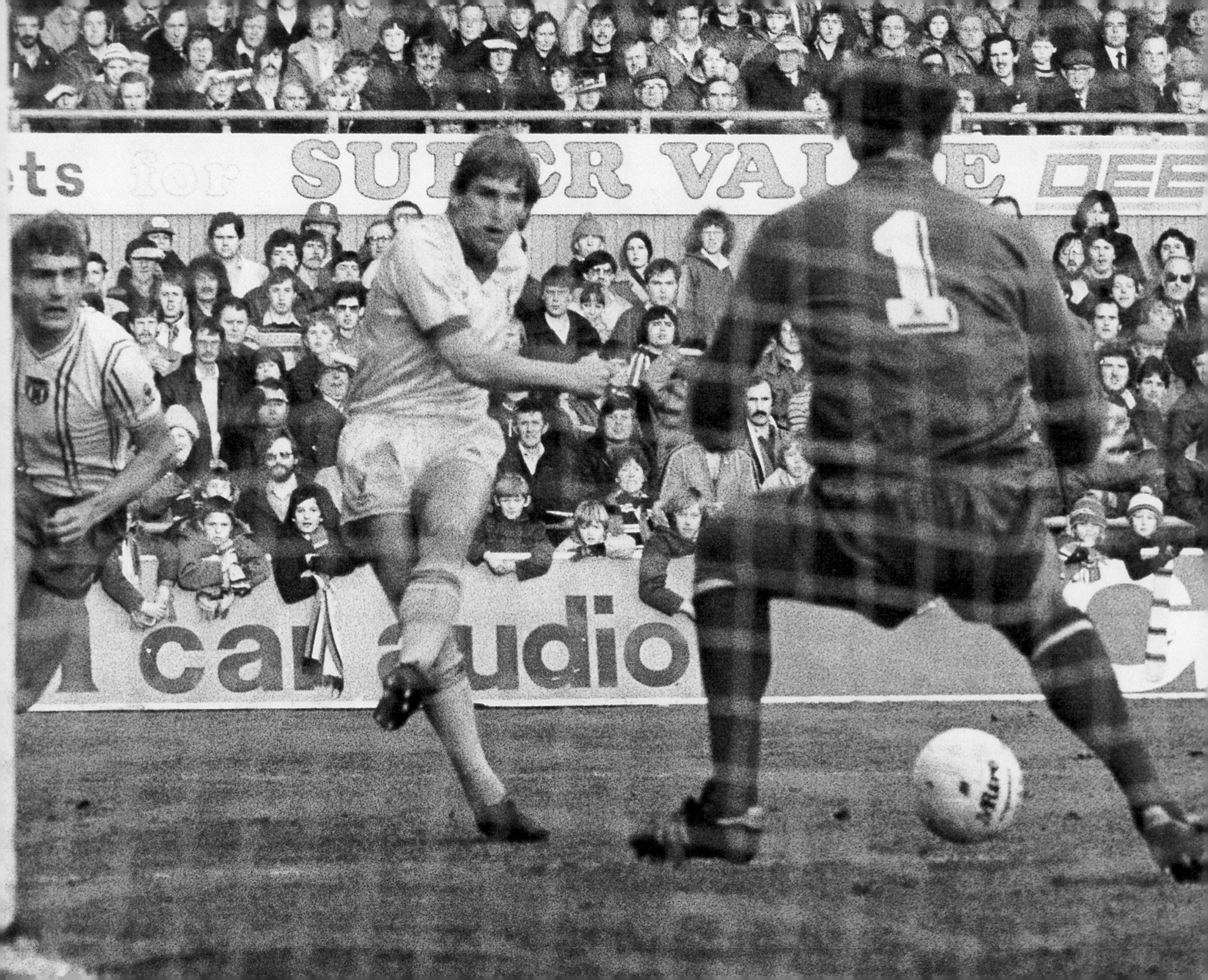

Goal Bound

No doubts about where this ball is heading!

Top Of The Table Manners

Never off duty, Bill Shankly talks team tactics. Toshack was the fork and Keegan the cream scone.

Skippy

Titi Camara takes on the Man Utd rearguard action in his stride.

All Smiles

From the start there were doubts whether job-share management had a part to play in the Premiership. The answer came four months later.

High Drama

Jason McAteer and Graham Stuart sum up the competitive spirit of a Merseyside derby.

Rare Sight

In a game against Sheffield Wednesday it's Ian Rush at his peak. Amazingly enough with his back to the goal.

Hello Boys

No prizes for guessing which team Him upstairs supports.

Heading For Goal

Ronnie Rosenthal scored a hat-trick on his debut. Not bad for a player Dalglish and Souness preferred to have on the subs bench.

Home James

David James attempts to
double his chances of getting
in the team – as keeper *and*
outfield player.

Muddy Waters

Fairclough, Hughes, Thompson, Case
and Heighway in the bath at Wolves
immediately after winning the League
title. John Toshack narrowly escaped
being dragged down the plug-hole.

Getting Shirty

The Chelsea defender didn't realise you were meant to swap shirts *after* the final whistle.

Under Control

Balance, natural ability and technique. Kenny Dalglish makes it look easy.

The One That Got Away

Terry McDermott takes time out from the action to talk fishing with team mate Jimmy Case during the Charity Shield match against West Ham.

previous page:

Typical

You wait ages for one trophy and then three come along at once.

Another Good Day At The Office

West Brom are the Anfield victims as Jimmy Case jumps for joy having scored from a deep midfield position.

Barking Mad

A goal down against Man Utd
and Phil Thompson and Gérard
Houllier reorganize in a bid to
get back on level terms.

Double Take

The four-man wall can't believe their
eyes and have to look at the scoreboard
again...Liverpool 4 Man Utd 0.

The Boss Man Ruling

Bob Paisley, as prepared as
ever for a pre-season friendly
over in Ireland.

Uncharitable Shield

A low point in his Liverpool career for
Kevin Keegan as he runs off for an
early bath at Wembley against Leeds.

Three Amigos

In the post-Hansen era Dalglish
adopted continental tactics for the
English game. Glenn Hysen, Ronnie
Whelan and Gary Gillespie form the
defensive flat back three.

Tight-lipped

Souness and Boersma are keeping quiet about their future after receiving the Board's vote of confidence.

Jubilation

An unlikely hero given the pedigree of the other players, yet Joey Jones enjoys a night out in Rome at the expense of German side Borussia Mönchengladbach.

Bottling It

After winning another League title, Graeme Souness and Terry McDermott try out the new team shampoo in the Anfield bath.

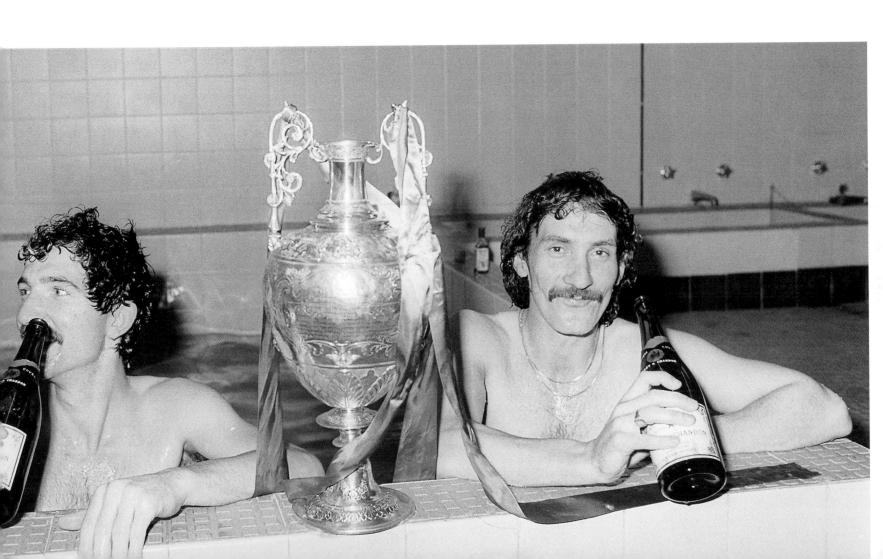

Trouble T'Mill

David Burrows takes matters
into his own hands as the
Leeds striker Eric Cantona
has some explaining to do.

Splish Splash

At the Nou Camp
in Barcelona you
got your own bath,
and that goes for
the physio too.

Retirement Day

Bob Paisley takes home more
than a cuckoo clock on his last
home game as manager. The
League title trophy was presented
prior to the Aston Villa game.

Can I Have My Ball Back?

Forest manager Brian Clough plays ballboy to Terry McDermott, symbolically handing over their League title hopes to Liverpool.

On Cue

It was rumoured The Tosh was so keen on pool he used to chalk the toe of his right boot before matches.

Dressed To Thrill

A 17-man wall prepares to defend the onslaught of stay press, crimplene and curling tongs. It was in fact clothing made to travel to the UEFA Cup final.

Space Age

At the time Astroturf was the answer to frozen and boggy pitches. When the irregular bounce appeared Jan Molby and the team were happy to turn their back on it.

Blown

It would become one of the most talked about matches ever (a game the BBC altered its Friday schedule to broadcast). For John Aldridge, great game, bad result.

previous page:

Bench Mark

Bob Paisley, Joe Fagan and Ronnie Moran are joined on the bench by a former landlord of The Rovers Return, Alec Gilroy, as they watch their side do battle in the lst leg of the European Cup semi-final against FC Zurich.

'Titi Camara. Action!'

Jamie Redknapp fills in some
time on the injury list by
moonlighting as a
cameraman for Sky TV.

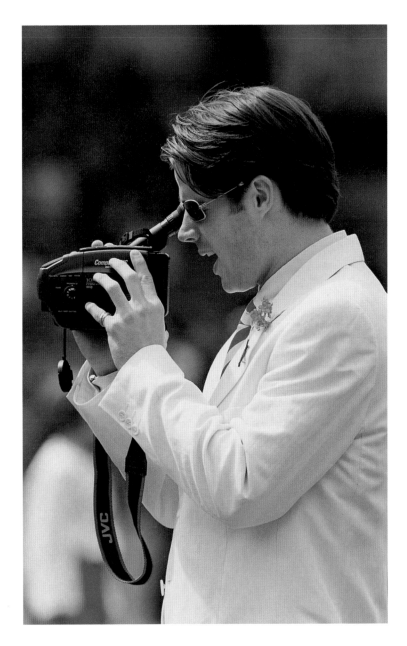

Star Studded

The stars of yesterday lend a hand to
the new crop of millennium talent. Little
Brian Hall, Peter McCormack and Emlyn
Hughes lead the applause.

Net Losses

It wasn't all fun and games for Terry McDermott, even though he did score twice in this game against Swansea.

Millennium Man

Deflated

The ball was seen as a symbol of Mark Wright and the team's fortunes in the early Premiership years.

You Have Been Well Red With ...

Thompson Flag (10 May 1978)
Tommy Smith (1 August 1968)
Spot On (8 November 1978)
Riding High (April 1995)
Ring…Ring… (May 1993)
Fan Power (December 1993)
Sweet FA (August 1974)
Before… (30 May 1984)
… And After (30 May 1984)
They Think It's All Over… (3 May 1986)
No Pushover (November 1996)
Table Football (1983)
In The Bag (20 May 1989)
Cool Customer (1986)
In His Stride (25 May 1977)
I Love You Too, Ref (November 1991)
Defender Of The Faith (21 November 1993)
King Of The Road (1974)
High Flyers (20 April 1992)
Doh! (3 November 1996)
Okay Lads, Here's The Plan (August 1999)
Berger King (28 August 1999)
In A Rush (March 1986)
Standing Room Only (23 April 1988)
Well Worth Watching (1977)
Try These For Size (October 1982)
All At Sea (1983)
Thanks For The Game, Son (9 March 1974)
Liver Birds (8 May 1971)
The Real Thing (July 1999)
Tongues Are Wagging (23 April 1988)
A Star Is Born (16 September 1998)
In Safe Hands (March 1973)
Standing Ovation (9 April 1988)
Tough At The Top ((25 April 1987)
'What's It Say, Brian?' (October 1972)
Home Alone (1996)
Walk On The Wild Side (1974)
Well Red (3 October 1993)
Fashion Victim (July 1994)

Danger: Low Flying Silverware (15 May 1982)
Walk This Way (20 May 1989)
Goal Bound (23 January 1982)
Top Of The Table Manners (1974)
Skippy (4 March 2000)
All Smiles (August 1998)
High Drama (November 1996)
Rare Sight (16 November 1986)
Heading For Goal (April 1991)
Hello Boys (1973)
Home James (August 1992)
Muddy Waters (4 May 1976)
Under Control (April 1981)
Getting Shirty (May 1986)
Typical (26 May 1977)
The One That Got Away (August 1980)
Another Good Day At The Office (27 August 1977)
Barking Mad (September 1999)
Double Take (16 September 1990)
The Boss Man Ruling (July 1980)
Uncharitable Shield (10 August 1974)
Three Amigos (November 1990)
Tight-lipped (September 1993)
Jubilation (25 May 1977)
Bottling It (May 1980)
Trouble T'Mill (18 April 1992)
Retirement Day (7 May 1983)
Splish Splash (March 1976)
Can I Have My Ball Back (28 April 1979)
Dressed To Thrill (May 1978)
On Cue (January 1976)
Blown (26 May 1989)
Space Age (January 1987)
Bench Mark (April 1977)
Star Studded (18 December 1999)
Titi Camara. Action! (May 1996)
Net Losses (3 October 1981)
Millennium Man (11 March 2000)
Deflated (August 1992)
Bill Shankly (10 August 1974)

First published in 2000 by Granada Media
an imprint of André Deutsch Ltd
76 Dean Street
London W1V 5HA
www.vci.co.uk

for Liverpool Football Club
in association with Granada Media Group

A catalogue record for this book is available from
the British Library

ISBN 0 233 99932 9

All photographs by Allsport, Empics, Hulton Getty,
Popperfoto, Andrew and John Varley and Simon
Buckley

Printed and bound in the UK by
Butler & Tanner, Frome and London

1 3 5 7 9 10 8 6 4 2